EARLY
SCIENCE

LIVING THING

KIM THOMPSON

A Crabtree Roots Book

Crabtree Publishing
crabtreebooks.com

School-to-Home Support for Caregivers and Teachers

This book helps children grow by letting them practice reading. Here are a few guiding questions to help the reader with building his or her comprehension skills. Possible answers appear here in red.

Before Reading:

• What do I think this book is about?
  • *I think this book is about plants and animals.*
  • *I think this book is about what makes something alive.*

• What do I want to learn about this topic?
  • *I want to learn if plants are alive just like animals.*
  • *I want to learn what living things do.*

During Reading:

• I wonder why...
  • *I wonder how other living things are like me.*
  • *I wonder if robots are alive.*

• What have I learned so far?
  • *I have learned that living things eat, drink, and breathe.*
  • *I have learned that living things have babies.*

After Reading:

• What details did I learn about this topic?
  • *I have learned that only some things are alive.*
  • *I have learned that all living things grow and have babies.*

• Read the book again and look for the vocabulary words.
  • *I see the word **food** on page 4 and the word **breathe** on page 6. The other vocabulary words are found on page 14.*

These are nonliving things.

Some things are **living things**.

Living things need **food** and water.

Nonliving things do not need food and water.

Living things **breathe**.

Nonliving things do not breathe.

Living things **grow**.

Nonliving things do not grow.

Living things have **babies**.

Nonliving things do not have babies.

Living things **move** on their own.

Nonliving things do not move on their own.

Word List
Sight Words

and	own
are	some
have	their
need	water
on	

Words to Know

babies   **breathe**   **food**

grow   **living things**   **move**

27 Words

Some things are **living things**.

Living things need **food** and water.

Living things **breathe**.

Living things **grow**.

Living things have **babies**.

Living things **move** on their own.

EARLY SCIENCE

LIVING THING

Written by: Kim Thompson

Designed by: Rhea Wallace

Series Development: James Earley

Proofreader: Kathy Middleton

Educational Consultant: Marie Lemke M.Ed.

Photographs:

Shutterstock: Locomotive74: cover; Alla Nurgaleera: p. 1; Lightfield Studios: p. 4; VladimirYa: p. 5; Daris Bastet Felis: p. 7; Rolling Rock: p. 7; 68inches of pleasure: p. 9; Vasiliy Budarin: p. 9b; Evelyn D. Harrison: p. 10; Tatjana Wagner: p. 11; Tatyaby: p. 12; Karelnoppe: p. 13

Crabtree Publishing

crabtreebooks.com   800-387-7650

Copyright © 2024 Crabtree Publishing

All rights reserved. No part of this publication may be reproduced, stored in a retrieval system or be transmitted in any form or by any means, electronic, mechanical, photocopying, recording, or otherwise, without the prior written permission of Crabtree Publishing.

Printed in the U.S.A./072023/CG20230214

Published in Canada
Crabtree Publishing
616 Welland Ave.
St. Catharines, Ontario
L2M 5V6

Published in the United States
Crabtree Publishing
347 Fifth Ave
Suite 1402-145
New York, NY 10016

Library and Archives Canada Cataloguing in Publication
Available at Library and Archives Canada

Library of Congress Cataloging-in-Publication Data
Available at the Library of Congress

Hardcover: 978-1-0398-0966-6
Paperback: 978-1-0398-1019-8
Ebook (pdf): 978-1-0398-1125-6
Epub: 978-1-0398-1072-3